Great Explorers

Discovering the New World

The Voyages of Christopher Columbus

Andrew Langley

Illustrated by Paul Crompton

Chelsea Juniors

A division of Chelsea House Publishers

Great Explorers
Discovering the New World
Exploring the Pacific
Journey into Space
The Great Polar Adventure

This edition published by Chelsea House
Publishers, a division of Main Line Book
Co., 300 Park Avenue South, New York,
New York 10010, by arrangement with
Irwin Jorvik Ltd.

© 1994 Irwin Jorvik Ltd.

© 1994 Chelsea House Publishers

All rights reserved.

1 3 5 7 9 8 6 4 2

ISBN 0-7910-2821-6

Contents

Born to the Sea

The year is 1492 and you are on a tiny wooden sailing ship journeying into unknown seas. It is three weeks since you left land and you are wondering whether you'll ever see your family and friends again. You don't trust your captain who thinks that you can travel west to reach the East. Many times you have asked him to turn the ship and take you home, but each time he refuses. His name is Christopher Columbus and this voyage is one that will soon make him one of the most famous explorers of all time.

Columbus was born in 1451 in the busy Italian port of Genoa. His father was a weaver and a wine merchant. As a young man he helped in his father's business, but his dearest wish was to go to sea. He probably made his first voyage when he was 14. At 19 he joined the crew of a galley and made many voyages around the Mediterranean, learning the art of seamanship.

In 1476, Columbus was sailing with a convoy bound for England. The convoy was attacked and his ship began to sink. He jumped overboard and swam ashore, clinging to an oar. He landed in Portugal.

Columbus made his way to Lisbon, the capital of Portugal, where he found a warm welcome. His brother, Bartholomew, lived in the city. Together, they set up a shop making and selling sea charts. Columbus married a Portuguese woman and learned to speak the language.

He also went back to sea. In the next few years he became a very skillful navigator and sailor. Soon he was captain of a Portuguese ship and sailed as far away as West Africa.

DID YOU KNOW?

Distances must have seemed very different to people in the fifteenth century. Sea travel was one of the few ways of traveling any great distance. West Africa would have seemed a world away to most European sailors, and the idea of traveling across an unknown ocean, out of sight of land for many weeks, was very frightening.

DID YOU KNOW?

Henry the Navigator (c. 1394-1460) was a Portuguese prince who helped make Portugal into a leading seafaring country. He never went on a voyage of exploration himself but he planned and paid for many voyages down the west coast of Africa. Thanks to him, sailing vessels, navigational instruments, and seafaring practices in general were greatly improved.

The Way to the East

Columbus had come to Portugal at an exciting point in history. For this was the great age of exploration by European voyagers.

In the 1400s, the people of Europe knew very little of the world. But they had heard of the adventures of men like Marco Polo. Polo was an Italian merchant who had reached China in 1275, after a journey across Asia that took him four years. When he returned in 1295, he told of the great wealth and wonderful cities of the East. He had the riches to prove it.

Jewels, silks, porcelain, and precious spices began to arrive in Europe. They were brought overland from Asia by traders. The goods were very expensive. Some Europeans wondered how they could obtain these treasures more cheaply and quickly. Perhaps they could find a route to the East by sea. The trouble was that nobody knew the way.

The Portuguese were the first to start looking for a sea route to Asia. Their little ships sailed southward along the west coast of Africa. Gradually, the expeditions went farther and farther.

Then at last, in 1487, Bartholomeu Dias sailed around the southernmost tip of Africa. He opened the way for a trading route to India, China, and the Spice Islands of the East.

DID YOU KNOW?

Spices were something that Columbus hoped to find on his voyages. Cloves, cinnamon, nutmeg, mace, and pepper are found in most kitchens today. But when Columbus was alive they were rare and very expensive. There were no refrigerators then and the spices were used to hide the taste of rotten meat! This map shows the overland route taken by spice traders from the East.

EUROPE   RUSSIA

Constantinople

TURKEY   Batumi   ASIA   Ninghsia

Tabriz   Kashgar   Shachow

Herat   Hindu Kush

Kerman   Himalayas   CHINA

INDIA

Indian Ocean   Bay of Bengal

PORTUGAL

AFRICA   INDIA

Atlantic Ocean

Indian Ocean

Cape of Good Hope

BARTHOLOMEU DIAS'S VOYAGE (Outward)

The Great Idea

Bartholomeu Dias sailed back into Lisbon harbor in 1488. Among the excited watchers on the quayside was Christopher Columbus. He, too, had read about Marco Polo's travels in Asia. He longed to see the marvels of Cathay and Cipango, as China and Japan were known then. Even more strongly he wanted to bring back their gold and other precious goods.

Columbus thought that the route to the East around Africa was much too long. He had his own amazing idea. Like many other people of the time, he knew that the world was round. So he decided to try a new route. Instead of going eastward, he would go westward and sail around the world to the East!

Columbus discussed his idea with scholars and mapmakers. One man told him that Cipango was only about 2,153 miles (5,600 km) to the west of Portugal. If he sailed in that direction, he would soon find land there. This was not true of course. Japan is actually 12,4000 miles (20,000 km) from Portugal. In between them are the huge continents of North America and South America.

Though the Vikings had reached North America nearly 500 years before, their settlements were soon abandoned and their discoveries never reported in western Europe. Columbus's plan was a brave one. At that time it was thought that no European ship had ever sailed so far to the west. It was a completely unknown region.

DID YOU KNOW?

Leif Eriksson, the Viking, was probably the first European to set foot in the New World. Around A.D. 1000 he led an expedition to the northeast coast of North America and established a settlement at a place he called Vinland. In 1968, this settlement was found in the part of Canada we now call Newfoundland.

The known world at the time of Columbus based on a map by Henricus Martellus, dated 1489.

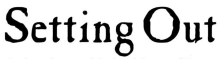

Setting Out

Columbus told the king of Portugal about his idea. He asked for ships and men. He also demanded to be made a nobleman and an admiral, and to have a share in the trade from the East.

The king was surprised at the boldness of the Genoese sailor. He called together a group of experts to decide on the matter. The experts rejected Columbus's plan. "It cannot be done!" they said.

In despair, Columbus left Portugal and went to Spain. He explained his project to the Spanish king, Ferdinand, and the queen, Isabella. At first they, too, would not agree to help him.

For five long years, Columbus tried to make them change their minds. At last, Ferdinand and Isabella agreed. They gave him three ships, and granted all his other wishes.

The little fleet left Palos in Spain, on August 3, 1492. Columbus sailed on the flagship, the *Santa María*. Behind came the two smaller vessels, the *Niña* and the *Pinta*.

The ships headed southward at first, and reached the Canary Islands. Here the sailors loaded on more stores and made repairs. On September 6 they set off again, going due west into the unknown. The great adventure had begun.

On Board the *Santa María*

Nobody knows exactly what Columbus's ships looked like. There are no pictures or descriptions of them. We can only make a guess by looking at other ships of the time.

Although the flagship *Santa María* was the biggest in Columbus's fleet, she was still very small compared with today's vessels. She was probably about 89 feet (27 m) long, with three masts carrying sails. All the ships were made of wood.

Life for the 40 men onboard was very harsh. Only Columbus had a cabin to himself. The other officers had tiny bunks, and the rest of the crew had to sleep on the open deck. This was difficult, because the deck sloped on each side. The only flat place was the hatch cover.

All the food was cooked on deck as well. The oven was a fire made in a special box protected from the wind and spray. The crew ate salted meat, hard biscuits, and dried peas, and drank water and wine.

Columbus had very few instruments to help him find the way. He was guided by a compass during the day, and at night by the stars. There were no clocks onboard. Instead, he used an hourglass. The sand took thirty minutes to run from top to bottom. Then it was turned over to measure the next half-hour.

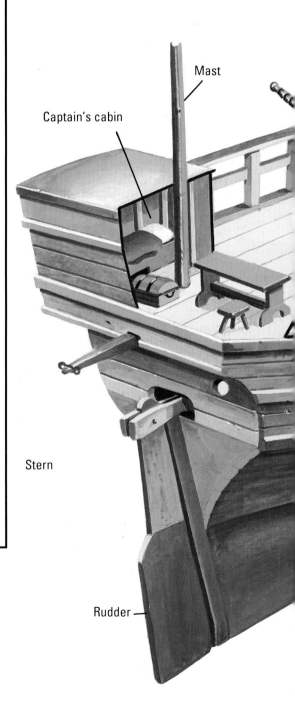

This is what a ship of Columbus's time would look like if you could see inside it.

Mast

Captain's cabin

Stern

Rudder

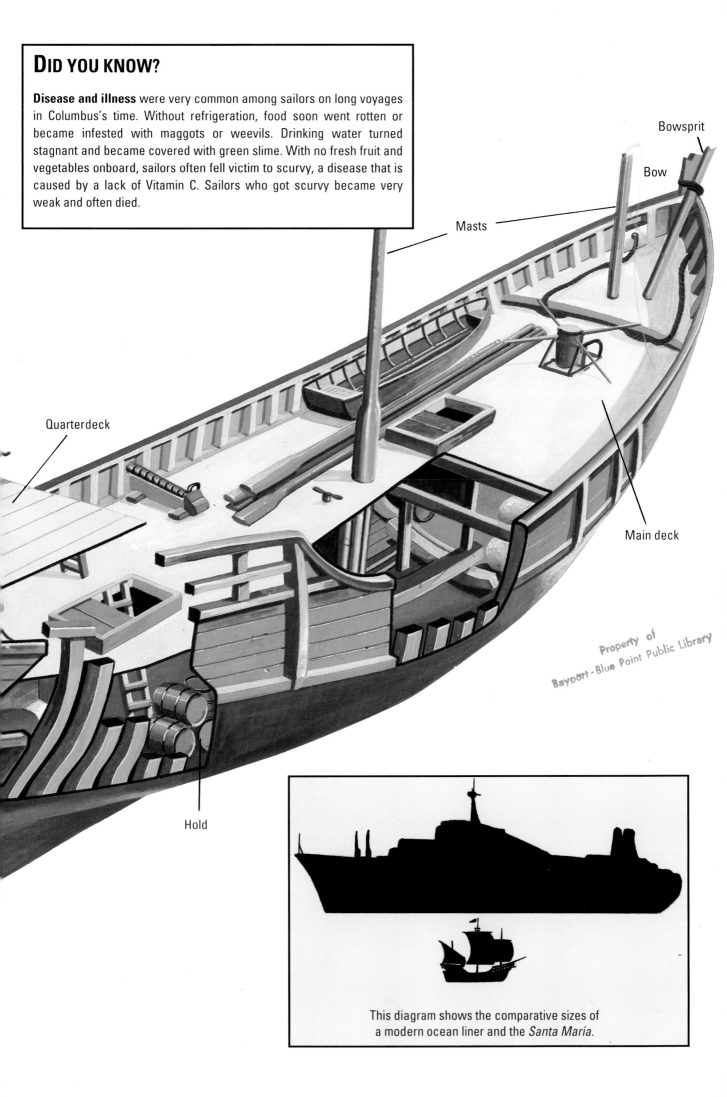

DID YOU KNOW?

Disease and illness were very common among sailors on long voyages in Columbus's time. Without refrigeration, food soon went rotten or became infested with maggots or weevils. Drinking water turned stagnant and became covered with green slime. With no fresh fruit and vegetables onboard, sailors often fell victim to scurvy, a disease that is caused by a lack of Vitamin C. Sailors who got scurvy became very weak and often died.

Bowsprit

Bow

Masts

Main deck

Quarterdeck

Hold

This diagram shows the comparative sizes of a modern ocean liner and the *Santa María*.

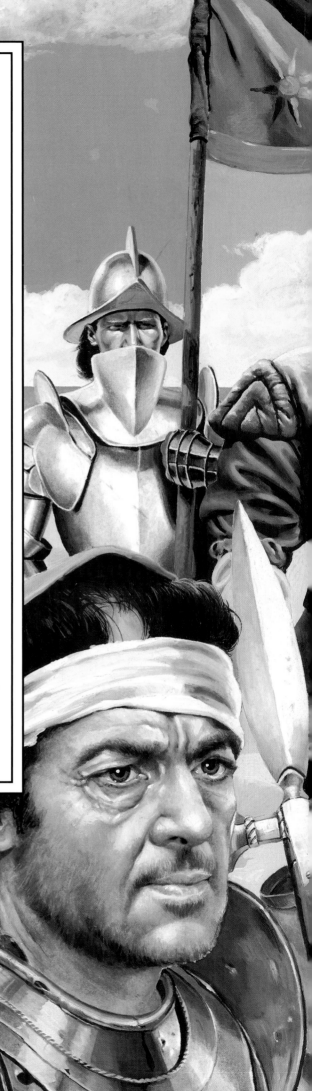

Land!

At first, the voyage went well. The sea was calm and the sun was warm. A good wind blew the ships onward. They sailed through the Sargasso Sea, where there were huge carpets of strange brown seaweed. Soon the men grew frightened. They had seen no land for three weeks. They would never get back to Spain again. They were lost!

Columbus did his best to calm them. They agreed to sail on for three more days. Then, if they found no land, they would turn back.

One day went by. Two days. At last, on October 12, they saw a white sandy cliff. 'Land! Land!' called the lookout. The ships had reached the islands we now call the Bahamas.

Columbus landed on the nearest island and named it San Salvador. He announced that it now belonged to Spain. The native people, called Arawaks, came to meet the explorers. They stared in amazement at their huge ships, their fine clothes, and their metal armor.

Columbus still believed that he was close to Cipango and the Spice Islands of the East Indies. So he soon sailed on again until he reached a much bigger island, modern-day Cuba. This, he thought, must be Cathay. His men went to search for gold mines and a great emperor, but all they found were small Arawak villages.

DID YOU KNOW?

The **Arawaks** were a peaceful, gentle-natured people who grew corn and yams for food. They wove cotton and made pottery. They slept in hammocks, an idea that the sailors copied. They were friendly to the explorers and keen to trade with them. Unfortunately, this did not prevent them from being virtually wiped out by the colonists.

NORTH AMERICA

COLUMBUS'S FIRST VOYAGE (Outward)

Spain

Atlantic Ocean

Azores

Portugal

Palos

Sargasso Sea

Canary Islands

Bahamas

Cuba

Hispaniola (Haiti/Dominican Republic)

AFRICA

Jamaica

Caribbean Sea

Trinidad

Venezuela

SOUTH AMERICA

Home Again

Columbus was still sure that Cipango and Cathay were very near. He sailed on to another big island. This was Haiti, which he named Hispaniola.

Here he found that the natives had a few small gold ornaments. They agreed to swap them for glass beads, shoes, and cloth. Columbus was very excited. Surely there were gold mines here!

Then came disaster. On Christmas Day the *Santa María* became stuck on a coral reef. She began to break up and sink. Columbus and his men scrambled ashore. The local chieftain helped them to rescue their food and belongings.

But how would they all get back to Spain? Columbus decided to build a fort on Hispaniola. He left 40 men there to explore and search for gold. On January 16, 1493, the rest of the party set off for Spain on the *Niña* and the *Pinta*.

The journey home was stormy and the two ships were almost sunk by the wind and waves. But somehow Columbus steered them back across the unknown ocean to the harbor at Palos in Spain.

Columbus and his officers rode in triumph across the country to Barcelona. They told King Ferdinand and Queen Isabella of their adventures. The king gave Columbus the title of Admiral of the Ocean Sea. He was now a rich and famous man.

DID YOU KNOW?

Tropical weather was a constant hazard for Columbus. It is usually hot and humid, making all work difficult. From June to November, there are often torrential downpours of rain as well as fierce hurricanes and other tropical storms.

Caribbean plants were very different from those familiar to Columbus. He believed that many of them could be cultivated and would be popular in Europe, and he was right. Tomatoes, maize, potatoes, beans, peanuts, peppers, cacao, pineapples, and many other food crops brought over from the New World are still enjoyed in Europe today.

COLUMBUS'S FIRST VOYAGE (Homeward)

NORTH AMERICA

Spain

Portugal

Azores

Palos

Atlantic Ocean

Canary Islands

Sargasso Sea

Bahamas

Cuba

Hispaniola (Haiti/Dominican Republic)

AFRICA

Jamaica

Caribbean Sea

Trinidad

Venezuela

SOUTH AMERICA

The Second Voyage

Columbus quickly began to organize a second expedition. This time, he was given a big fleet. There were 17 ships carrying about 1,000 men and 50 horses. The voyage had three aims. One was to found colonies on the islands. Another was to convert the local tribes to the Christian faith. And the third? To find gold, of course!

The fleet sailed on September 25, 1493. It made a quick and easy crossing of the Atlantic, and soon reached the fort on Hispaniola. It was deserted! The Spanish settlers had been cruel to the native Arawaks. So the Arawaks had killed them all and destroyed the fort. Columbus founded a new colony nearby, which he called Isabella.

Then he set off by sea to explore the coastline of Cuba. He was still looking for Cipango and Cathay. All he found was a new island, Jamaica.

When he returned to Isabella, the new colony, there was more trouble. The Spaniards were fighting each other. They were short of food and were stealing from the local people, who rebelled and refused to work for them.

Columbus led an army against the Arawaks. He easily defeated them and put many to death. He hoped that the colony would now live in peace. In 1496 he sailed back to Spain, taking several natives with him as slaves.

DID YOU KNOW?

Horses were unknown in the New World until brought there by the European settlers. Horses later completely changed the lifestyle of the North American Plains Indians, who used them to chase down the herds of buffalo that the Indians hunted for food and clothing.

COLUMBUS'S SECOND VOYAGE

NORTH AMERICA

Spain

Portugal

Azores

Palos

Atlantic Ocean

Sargasso Sea

Canary Islands

Bahamas

Cuba

Hispaniola (Haiti/Dominican Republic)

AFRICA

Jamaica

Caribbean Sea

Trinidad

Venezuela

SOUTH AMERICA

The Third Voyage

Columbus once again went to see Ferdinand and Isabella. He showed them the gold and slaves he had brought back. It was not very much, but he still believed that the riches of the East were very near.

The king and queen agreed to another expedition. In 1498, Columbus set off again with 6 vessels. He sent 3 of them straight to Hispaniola. With the others he traveled further south.

He hoped to find a land with more gold, but instead he found the Doldrums. These are parts of the ocean round the Equator where there is often no wind and ships are becalmed, or unable to move.

After eight long days the wind sprang up again. They sailed on to Trinidad and the coast of Venezuela. Columbus had at last reached the mainland of South America. He called it the "Other World."

The ships then sailed on to Hispaniola. The settlers there were very angry. They had found no gold, and did not know how to grow food. They had also killed most of the natives or made them into slaves.

Columbus was unable to control them. By 1500, King Ferdinand had heard about the violence and disorder in his new colony. He sent an envoy to Hispaniola. The envoy put Columbus in chains and shipped him back to Spain in disgrace.

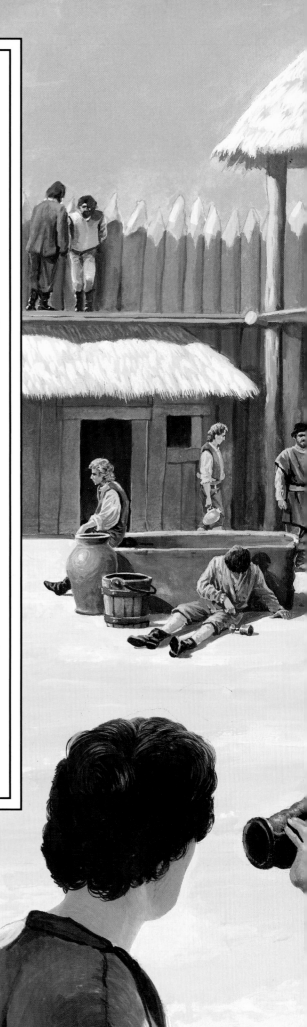

COLUMBUS'S THIRD VOYAGE

NORTH AMERICA

Atlantic Ocean

Sargasso Sea

Bahamas

Cuba

Hispaniola (Haiti/Dominican Republic)

Jamaica

Caribbean Sea

Trinidad

Venezuela

SOUTH AMERICA

Azores

Spain

Portugal

Palos

Canary Islands

AFRICA

The Last Chance

Columbus had by this time made three voyages to the Caribbean. He had not found what he wanted. There was little gold, and no spices or other riches. There was no sign of the great Emperor of Cathay.

Columbus begged King Ferdinand to give him one last chance. On May 9, 1502, he set sail with four vessels. He hoped to find a way through the islands and into the Indian Ocean.

When he reached Hispaniola, Columbus realized that a hurricane was coming. He warned the king's envoy on the island, but the envoy laughed at him and sent a big fleet to sea. The hurricane roared down, destroying the fleet and sinking twenty ships.

Columbus's vessels were saved. They sailed on to Honduras, then down the coast of Central America. On they fought through storms and rain, but they found no way through.

The ships were leaking badly, so Columbus left two behind and headed for Jamaica. Here the two remaining ships went aground.

Columbus and his men were marooned for a whole year. They argued with each other and were very short of food. At last, in June 1504, they were rescued and taken back to Spain.

Columbus was now very ill, worn out by his travels. He died in Valladolid, Spain, in May 1506. He had never reached Asia, but he had found a new continent. It was not named after him, however. Instead, mapmakers called it America after the explorer, Amerigo Vespucci.

COLUMBUS'S FOURTH VOYAGE

NORTH AMERICA

Spain

Portugal

Palos

Atlantic Ocean

Azores

Sargasso Sea

Canary Islands

Bahamas

Cuba

Hispaniola (Haiti/Dominican Republic)

AFRICA

Jamaica

Caribbean Sea

Trinidad

Venezuela

SOUTH AMERICA

DID YOU KNOW?

Amerigo Vespucci was an Italian merchant and navigator. Between 1499 and 1502 he made two voyages to South America and established that Columbus had sailed to a new continent to the west of Europe, and not to China and Japan in the East. In 1507, a German mapmaker produced a map in which the newly discovered lands were called America in honour of Vespucci.

After Columbus

When Columbus had first come to Hispaniola, there were about 3 million people living there. Ten years later, there were only 30,000 left. In the end, all the island's natives were wiped out.

Many other Europeans quickly followed Columbus across the Atlantic. Their search for wealth brought nothing but misery and death for the native peoples.

In 1519 Hernán Cortés landed in Mexico. With a small army he destroyed the mighty empire of the Aztecs. Other Spanish invaders conquered the rest of Central America. They seized its riches and sent them back to Spain.

Next, the Europeans turned to South America. In 1531 Francisco Pizarro marched into the Inca empire with only 177 men. His cannons and guns killed thousands of Incas. Soon, he had conquered the whole of Peru.

In exchange for its plundered riches, the invaders brought deadly diseases and slavery to the New World. The Indians were forced to work growing crops or mining for gold and silver. Most of them died or ran away.

By the early 1600s, the English, Dutch, and French had started colonies on the islands of the Caribbean. They wanted to grow sugarcane. Because nearly all the native Indian tribes had been destroyed, the settlers brought slaves from Africa. Over the next 250 years, twelve million Africans were captured and brought to the Caribbean, and North America and South America. Nearly two million died on the voyage. Millions more died young because of the hard work in very bad conditions on the plantations. Meanwhile, their owners grew wealthy and powerful.

DID YOU KNOW?

The Aztecs had a legend that one of their gods - Quetzalcoatl - would return to them from across the seas. When Hernán Cortés arrived off the east coast of Mexico in 1519, the Aztec emperor, Montezuma II, did nothing to stop him, believing that Cortés was the god himself. Two years later, the Spanish completely destroyed the Aztec Empire.

A Sad History

Most of today's population in Central America and South America is of mixed descent from all the people who came to the continent – Spanish, British, Portuguese, French, Dutch, and African, as well as the native people. They are no longer slaves but most of them are very poor.

The Bahamas, where Columbus first landed, are a famous holiday resort. Hispaniola is now two countries, called Haiti and the Dominican Republic. Most of the people there are peasant farmers and their most important crops are still sugar and coffee.

Gold and silver are still mined in Mexico. But most Mexicans work on tiny farms. Much of the land is dry and rocky and crops do not grow well.

The whole region has a sad and violent history. Civil wars and terrorism help to keep the countries poor by destroying farmland and factories.

Yet we cannot blame Columbus for everything that has happened there. His bravery and navigational skills opened the way to the New World and helped make both Europe and North America the rich and powerful continents that they are today.

His name is remembered across North America and South America. Colombia is named after him. Many towns and cities across North America are called Columbus, and the U.S. capital, Washington, lies in the District of Columbia.